LOVE

and

HATE

ROBERT ROGERS

Author's Tranquility Press
MARIETTA, GEORGIA

Robert Rogers/Author's Tranquility Press
2706 Station Club Drive SW
Marietta, GA 30060
www.authorstranquilitypress.com

Ordering Information:
Quantity sales. Special discounts are available on quantity purchases by corporations, associations, and others. For details, contact the "Special Sales Department" at the address above.

Love and Hate/Robert Rogers
Hardback: 978-1-959453-25-3
Paperback: 978-1-959453-26-0
eBook: 978-1-959453-27-7

CONTENTS

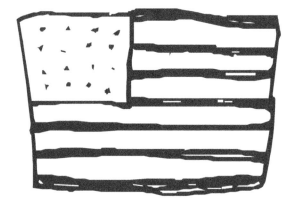

A Divided World

The world we're in causes grief
We search for relief
It's hard to know what is true
What can we do?

We hear thousands of words
Those words often conflict with how we feel
Those words are unpredictable
And don't become real

Once they did
Now they don't
There Is a great divide
We collide

Countries struggle and strive
Peace may never arrive
We continue the divide
And live with the grief

Search to learn what will be
We shall see
Remain together or apart
Where do we start?

No-one seems to know
Those divided feelings seem to grow
They cause hatred and disbelief
Will we ever see relief?

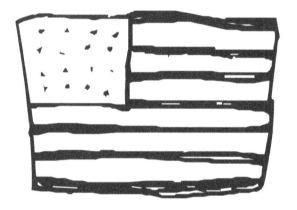

The world is moving at a hectic pace
Who will win the race?
We may never reach the end
We ask ourselves when

We may never know

A Loving Chance

When we first met, she gently held my hand and smiled
I asked her to dance
I wanted to hold her close but
I didn't want to take the chance

I could see the glow in her eyes
I was surprised
I held her close and we danced

The music played but I could barely hear the sound
She held mc tight and whispered in my ear
She said she loved to dance
I thought there might be a chance

When the music stopped, I held her close
We slowly walked back to a chair
I didn't let go and she didn't seem to care
Without touching our hearts seemed to dance
I knew I had a chance

I said I had some
Country records she might like to hear
She smiled and said
I'm a country girl and like those sounds
I thought I might have a chance

I played those records and
She lovingly looked at me and said
I'm a country girl and like it that way
I didn't know what to say

I could see that glow in her eyes
I was surprised
I took her hand and pulled her close
She said I'd love to dance

We held each other tight
We both knew this was right
I could barely hear the sound
I knew that loving chance finally came around

COUNTRY

I like the country
Not Kansas
The music
Three cords paint the truth

Country speaks to all
Tell us what we were
The words are clear
Tell us how we got here

They tell a story
About things we know
Remind us who we were
They circle back to our beginning

The acoustic guitar and the mandolin
That's where country began
It's the lyrics that entice
They promise shining hearts or thunder strikes

Country songs never die
"I'm so lonesome I could cry"
A country of broken hearts and hope
They simply tell the truth

The songs come in all languages
In Spanish?
Guantanamera
Country has "A coat of many colors"

The music comes with creative sounds
But country will always be around
It reminds us who we are
The history of life

Country will never end
Circle back to our beginning
Times that will live forever
As we sing together

Get the guitar or mandolin
Play the songs again
They tell us how we live and die "
A country still unbroken"

HARD TO BE ALONE

It's hard to be alone
I live in a cold, cold home
Once the fires burned bright
Now I live in the rain

The sun no longer shines
You left and are no longer mine
I still linger for your touch
I loved you so much

I can't hold you again
My heart brakes when I think of you
You left when I needed you
I can't do this again

My life has an empty place
Your love is no longer mine
That fire is gone
I am alone

I shall live with what I once knew
I will no longer see you
Your memory will linger a long time
You are not mine

That fire will no longer burn
Our love will not return
You live a different life
I will be alone

I have a loving memory
I don't know why you left me
You opened the door and walked away
I didn't know what to say

I should have warmed by your side
And helped that fire burn bright
Known what was right
I let the fire die

LOVE FALLS APART

Our love has fallen apart
I don't know where to start
The loving was intense
Strange things have happened since

Maybe it's something we did
Or didn't do
What's true?
It's hard to say

We both made mistakes
I regret the games we played
It causes heart aches
I followed the game

I thought we still had a chance
We live in a world of circumstance
Love can change
Our love has fallen apart

When falling to the ground
It made little sound
That loving embrace has faded
We both have made mistakes

I wish I could change what I have done
Alter the games we both played
Search for the love we once had
We both have made mistakes

Your love remains in my heart
Forgotten what real love takes
We have made mistakes
Our feelings may never blend

I think we have reached the end
We may never meet again
And listen to our hearts
And know what loving takes

We've made mistakes

She Loves Me

She loves me I know
She told me so
Why I just don't know
It's unknown

It must be sexual desire or affection
Tenderness
I can only guess
That feeling I cherish

A rose loves sunlight
So, do I
I want to see that flower glow
Her reason to love I want to know

I hold her hand and look in her eyes
The sunlight shines
That love is mine
I can't decline

We walk a narrow line
Love is how we feel
It's hard to know what is real
We shall see
She says she loves me

Love has its changes
It may burn bright
Love can change in time
That loving sunlight can darken

Linger in darkness
Only shadows remain
We will walk that fine line
See what happens in time

She says
I will love you until that distant sun no longer shines

THE SIDEWALK

I'd like to see you again
Meet me on the sidewalk
We can walk among the lights
And talk again

I love that red dress you wear
I want to walk with you somewhere
The sidewalk seems the place
I want you to know I care

I've known you for a very short time
That longing feeling is mine
As we walk, I see the sunshine in your hair
I want to know you for a much longer time

The wind blows that flowing red dress
You don't care
As we walk down the sidewalk
I'm glad you're there

Our talk is sweet
Your eyes glow brighter under the lights
The sidewalk is our place to be
I'm glad you walk with me

We will slowly walk
And talk about the things we like
And wonder what might be
We shall see

THE WAITING WORLD

How do we change this waiting world?
Do we simply wait and see?
We will soon find what it will be
Maybe a world that remains under the glowing stars

Or a world that grows cold
And we can no longer see a rainbow
We simply don't know
We may live with darkened stars

Heaven seems to have a lingering pace
Our world has a faster race
We don't know why
We simply don't try

When we no longer see the rainbow
We may search for its light
It may never be in sight
What is right?

We don't seem to know
Just accept its disappearing glow.
Heaven changing is slow
But our world is vastly moving

There are other worlds
They may still have rainbows
It will take a while
Heaven may show us the way

We really can't say
We don't know the way
We search for those other worlds
Finding them may give us hope

Heaven may give us a different world
With bright stars and rainbows

WAR IS HELL

War is hell
You may not have been there
But you must know how I feel
That feeling still remains

When I sleep war recurs
I wake feeling bad
I stumble through the darkness
I remember those feeling I once had

I cling to the door
I open it to see if the world has changed
It hasn't
My sad feelings remain

I search for the answer
I turn on a light
I want to remember what is right
War is hell

When will I be well?
Only time will tell
How do I lose those feelings?
I live in hell

As I grow older
The search takes its toll
Opening that door sheds no light
The world is no longer bright
War was hell

I think Seeger was right
"Where Have All the Soldiers Gone?
Gone for Graveyards Everyone.
When Will They Ever learn?"

I will search for the flowers

UNCHARTED WORLD

I live in an uncharted world
I linger in love
I dream
My life is like a drifting soul

I wish my dream would unfold
Open with a woman to lovingly hold
But dreams are not true
I just linger in love

We live in different worlds
That's why my dreams can't come true
They don't linger
They drift in an uncharted world

What shall I do?
I really don't know
Perhaps I'll just close my eyes
And wish my dream will come true

I want to share my love
Love is contagious
It infects our souls
And makes us want the love

I close my eyes and feel her warmth
It makes me smile
And lingers for awhile
But I know my dream can't be true

When I open my eyes
I know I've been drifting in an uncharted world
But I can still see her smile
It lingers for awhile

Someday my dream may come true
I will hold her and feel her touch
I will know my dream is true
I will have found my dream in this uncharted world

I'm Alone

I'm Alone
I have always been this way
I live alone
That feeling just seems to stay

A pretty woman found me
She wanted me to change
That goal seemed to be her plight
I don't know why

She thought her effort was right
I just couldn't comply
I did try
She went away

She decided to refrain
Just let me be alone
Her eyes filled with tears
As she slowly walked out the door

She didn't see me anymore
What a fool I must have been
I'm alone again
She closed the door

I struggle to see the light
Find a woman who can rekindle my plight?
Let her open that door
I know being alone isn't right

What shall I do?
I'm alone
I search for that change
It may not come true

I may always be alone

No Longer Mine

Barbara is no longer mine
I may never see your eyes shine
I close my eyes and remember what was mine
You went away and dark clouds came

We were once the same
We loved the dance
I laughed and you held my hand
That loving light was bright

Where can I go from here?
I hang my head and see you clear
That sunshine is no longer here
Dark clouds remain

I want to see your eyes again
Revel in the sunlight
And remember what was mine
I want to hold you

That will never be
I think you are unkind
Your bright love is gone
Darkness remains

That darkness wraps like chains
I can't escape
It locks me in this darkness
The key is no longer in sight

You are no longer mine
The sun doesn't shine
Rain replaces what we once had
Barbara I will no longer hold you

I close my eyes and walk in the rain

I'm Still Alive

I don't know why I'm still alive
I'm 82 and I still survive
The grandkids seek my advice
A mistake

The world has changed
My old thoughts and ideas remain
They needn't be reclaimed
They are old

Old doesn't mean it's better
It's just a feeling many have
The older we get the less clarity we see
We are often blind

Some think old is right
What do they really know?
Seeking advice is a noble cause
They want to know

It was a life of love and regret
I still don't know what will happen yet
Wars were everlasting
I remember them well

War was hell
The woman I loved is still here
She waited for me
Why I really can't tell

I struggled in a jungle of vines and wire
It was much like home
In a different place
The grandkids will never know

I can't tell them what 82 is like
A life they may never know
That iPhone could make it so
What a change

They can look at the world with a simple click
And discover a different cast
82 won't last
It simply can list a long-remembered past

I'm a little concerned why they can't read her letters
Or read the clock, just a concern of mine
I'm 82 I know what life is like
Their life is not like mine

Can they sign their name?

CPSIA information can be obtained
at www.ICGtesting.com
Printed in the USA
BVHW061055110123
655995BV00019BB/1254